For EL,

My MEISTERWERK!

MANY HAPPY RETURNS

with love

hyun

21. 3. 22

ULTIMUTTS

ULTIMUTTS

A Celebration of Street Dogs and Strays

Edited by Wynn Wheldon

MQP

MUTTS

How do we define a mutt? Well, it is perhaps easier to say what a mutt is not. A mutt will never win a fancy dog show, nor can it be a police dog, a rescue dog, or a guide dog. A mutt doesn't enjoy herding sheep. In other words, there is nothing very useful about a mutt. Then again a mutt is very far from being a lap dog. A mutt is emphatically not a toy.

What a mutt has above all is an aura of independence, of individuality. It can roam the streets of Calcutta, unclaimed by anyone, or it can ignore its keeper's vain shouts among the trees and bushes of the local park.

A mutt has a look in which the human can actually see the thought taking place: "Shall I or shan't I?". The mutt weighs up the pros and cons. There is no blind obedience here, for the mutt is a savvy creature, often streetwise, about as far from dull and stupid as it is possible to be. A mutt chooses its own activity. This, on the whole, consists of lying around doing nothing at all. Idleness, of a positively Aristotelian nobility, is a marked quality of the mutt, and so mutts get on terrifically well with hippies, poets, and tramps. A mutt is a loose dog, a freedom-loving dog, a liberal dog.

Mutts have to have muttish monikers. You cannot really call a mutt Anubis or Cerberus or Sirius or Xolotl, for example. These are far too grand for mutts. Nor would they want them. They are much happier with Boots or Ruff or Fred or Tramp or Scamp or Scruff or Patch or Tyke. In other words, they suit a monosyllable, with perhaps the occasional diminutive "-y" suffix, although that tends to lead to the horrors of the cute.

Above all they suggest something lovable, and although it is true that you are more likely to be bitten by a poodle than a mongrel, there is about the mutt something Other. Dogs are man's best friend, faithful to the end, symbolic of this, that, and the other, but the mutt retains a last vestige in this most domesticated of all species, of the wild. This does not make it savage or dangerous; indeed rather than any negative connotation, we are more inclined to suggest that it is the mutt that gives modern, urban man his most direct connection to nature—the mutt is something to be treasured, but never ever put into a tartan winter coat.

There will always be a lost dog somewhere that will prevent me from being happy.

Jean Anouilh

SYMPATHY FOR UNGAINLY DOGS

I have all my life had a sympathy for mongrel, ungainly dogs, who are nobody's pets; and I would rather surprise one of them by a pat and a pleasant morsel, than meet the condescending advances of the loveliest Skye terrier who has his cushion by my lady's chair.

George Eliot *Scenes from Clerical Life*

If only men could love each other like dogs, the world would be paradise.

James Douglas

A SAGACIOUS DOG

In Hungary, as elsewhere, there are dogs of kindly nature and gentle culture. I can record a curious instance of reasoning power in a dog named "Jockey," who is well known at Buda Pest. He has the habit of crossing over the Pest to Buda every morning of his life in one or another of the little steamboats that ply backwards and forwards. He regularly takes his walk over there, and then returns as before by steamer. This is his practice in summer; but when winter arrives, and the ice on the Danube stops the traffic of the steamboats, then Jockey has recourse to the bridge.

Andrew F. Crosse *Round About the Carpathians*

PATRASCHE

But the old man was very gentle and good to the boy, and the boy was a beautiful, innocent, truthful, tender-hearted creature; and they were happy on a crust and a few leaves of cabbage, and asked no more of earth or heaven; save indeed that Patrasche should be always with them, since without Patrasche where would they have been?

For Patrasche was their alpha and omega; their treasury and granary; their store of gold and wand of wealth; their bread-winner and minister; their only friend and comforter. Patrasche dead or gone from them, they must have laid themselves down and died likewise. Patrasche was body, brains, hands, head, and feet to both of them: Patrasche was their very life, their very soul. For Jehan Daas was old and a cripple, and Nello was but a child; and Patrasche was their dog.

Ouida *A Dog of Flanders*

If a dog's prayers were answered, bones would rain from the sky.

Proverb

MR. SIKES'S DOG

In the obscure parlour of a low public-house, in the filthiest part of Little Saffron Hill; a dark and gloomy den, where a flaring gas-light burnt all day in the winter-time; and where no ray of sun ever shone in the summer: there sat, brooding over a little pewter measure and a small glass, strongly impregnated with the smell of liquor, a man in a velveteen coat, drab shorts, half boots and stockings, who even by that dim light no experienced agent of police would have hesitated to recognise as Mr. William Sikes. At his feet sat a white-coated, red-eyed dog; who occupied himself, alternately, in winking at his master with both eyes at the same time; and in licking a large, fresh cut on one side of his mouth, which appeared to be the result of some recent conflict.

"Keep quiet, you warmint! Keep quiet!" said Mr. Sikes, suddenly breaking silence. Whether his meditations were so intense as to be disturbed by the dog's winking, or whether his feelings were so wrought upon by his reflections that they required all the relief derivable from kicking an unoffending animal to allay them, is matter for argument and consideration.

Whatever was the cause, the effect was a kick and a curse, bestowed upon the dog simultaneously.

Dogs are not generally apt to revenge injuries inflicted upon them by their masters; but Mr. Sikes's dog, having faults of temper in common with his owner, and labouring, perhaps, at this moment, under a powerful sense of injury, made no more ado but at once fixed his teeth in one of the half-boots. Having given in a hearty shake, he retired, growling, under a form; just escaping the pewter measure which Mr. Sikes levelled at his head.

"You would, would you?" said Sikes, seizing the poker in one hand, and deliberately opening with the other a large clasp-knife, which he drew from his pocket. "Come here, you born devil! Come here! D'ye hear?"

The dog no doubt heard; because Mr. Sikes spoke in the very harshest key of a very harsh voice; but appearing to entertain some unaccountable objection to having his throat cut, he remained where he was, and growled more fiercely than before: at the same time grasping the end of the poker between his teeth, and biting at it like a wild beast.

This resistance only infuriated Mr. Sikes the more; who, dropping on his knees, began to assail the animal most furiously. The dog jumped from right to left, and from left to right; snapping, growling, and barking; the man thrust and swore, and struck and blasphemed; and the struggle was reaching a most critical point for one or other; when, the door suddenly opening, the dog darted out: leaving Bill Sikes with the poker and the clasp-knife in his hands.

There must always be two parties to a quarrel, says the old adage. Mr. Sikes, being disappointed of the dog's participation, at once transferred his share in the quarrel to the new comer.

Charles Dickens *Oliver Twist*

Rambunctious, rumbustious, delinquent dogs become angelic when sitting.

Dr. Ian Dunbar

KASHTANKA

Kashtanka ran up and down and did not find her master, and meanwhile it had got dark. The street lamps were lighted on both sides of the road, and lights appeared in the windows. Big, fluffy snowflakes were falling and painting white the pavement, the horses' backs and the cabmen's caps, and the darker the evening grew the whiter were all these objects. Unknown customers kept walking incessantly to and fro, obstructing her field of vision and shoving against her with their feet. (All mankind Kashtanka divided into two uneven parts: masters and customers; between them there was an essential difference: the first had the right to beat her, and the second she had the right to nip by the calves of their legs.)

These customers were hurrying off somewhere and paid no attention to her.

When it got quite dark, Kashtanka was overcome by despair and horror. She huddled up in an entrance and began whining piteously. The long day's journeying with Luka Alexandritch had exhausted her, her ears and her paws were freezing, and, what was more, she was terribly hungry. Only twice in the whole day had she tasted a morsel: she had eaten a little paste at the bookbinder's, and in one of the taverns she had found a sausage skin on the floor, near the counter— that was all. If she had been a human being she would have certainly thought: "No, it is impossible to live like this!"

Anton Chekhov *Kashtanka*

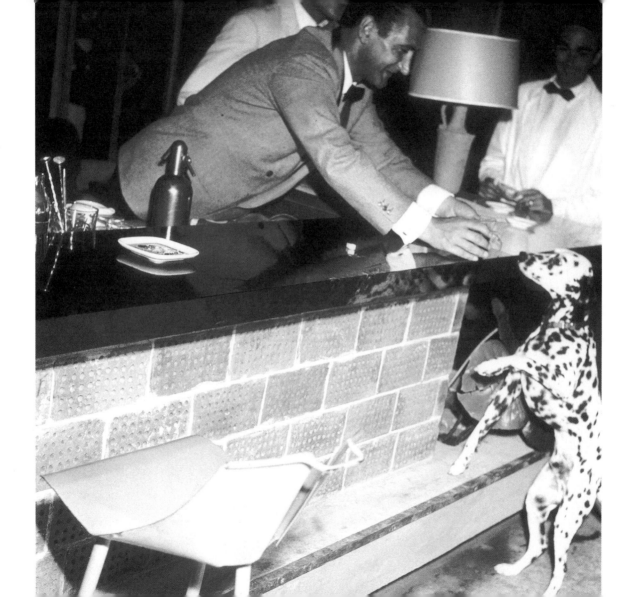

A STRAY DOG

A stray dog, sniffing about, came up to me. Generally, I dislike dogs and beasts of all kinds. I called this one in, and gave him his supper. He had been taught (I suppose) to sit up on his hind legs, and beg for food: at any rate, this was his way of asking me for more, I laughed—it seems impossible when I look back at it now, but for all that it's true—I laughed till the tears ran down my cheeks, at the little beast on his haunches, with his ears pricked up, and his head on one side, and his mouth watering from the victuals. I wonder whether I was in my right senses? I don't know. When the dog had got all he could get, he whined to be let out to roam the streets again.

Wilkie Collins *Man and Wife*

DOGS AND THE OCEAN

To see a little trembling dainty-footed cur stand on the margin of the ocean, and ineffectually bark at the beach-bird, amid the roar of the Atlantic! Come with design to bark at a whale, perchance! That sound will do for farmyards. All the dogs looked out of place there, naked and as if shuddering at the vastness; and I thought that they would not have been there had it not been for the countenance of their masters. I used to see packs of half-wild dogs haunting the lonely beach on the south shore of Staten Island, in New York Bay, for the sake of the carrion there cast up; and I remember that once, when for a long time I had heard a furious barking in the tall grass of the marsh, a pack of half a dozen large dogs burst forth on to the beach, pursuing a little one which ran straight to me for protection, and I afforded it with some stones, though at some risk to myself; but the next day the little one was the first to bark at me.

Henry David Thoreau *The Sea and the Desert*

THE TOWN PUMP

This thirsty dog, with his red tongue lolling out, does not scorn my hospitality, but stands on his hind legs, and laps eagerly out of the trough.

Nathaniel Hawthorne *A Rill from the Town Pump*

ABOUT DOGS

I send this article to you hoping that the city authorities will find it a duty to come to our immediate relief. A convention of dogs nightly congregate in a certain locality on Auburn street, and make the night hideous with their growling and fighting, and greatly annoy the peaceable inhabitants of that locality. Some sentimental saphead has said, "Let dogs delight to bark and bite," as I do not find this sublime stanza in either Blackstone or Mother Goose, I am not willing to accept it as the Common Law of the land, and am inclined to think it possesses more of a theological than legal meaning.

Whether these dogs convene for the purpose of conspiring against the rest of the inhabitants in the neighborhood, or whether it is to discuss the all-important feminine question, I am unable to state.

It is certain that they meet, however, great dogs and small dogs; the thoroughbred of the aristocrat, and the common cur of the plebeian, all meet upon an equal footing—truly a most Democratic assemblage. The writer of this has exhausted all the ordinary means of private citizen in order to bring peace to the afflicted denizens of the locality. I have thrown old boots and evacuated slippers, my last bar of hard soap, and every available missile to be found in the back yard of a well regulated boarding house. I now desire to call the attention of the proper authorities to this dogged nuisance, and hope we shall not be driven to the desperate necessity of administering sedatives to these dogs in person in self-defence.

Caroline M. Churchill Little Sheaves

Well-washed and well-combed domestic pets grow dull; they miss the stimulus of fleas.

Francis Galton

**I do not ask you much,
I beg cold comfort.**

William Shakespeare *King John*

LONE DOG

I'm a lean dog, a keen dog, a wild dog and lone;
I'm a rough dog, a tough dog, hunting on my own;
I'm a bad dog, a mad dog, teasing silly sheep;
I love to sit and bay the moon and keep fat souls from sleep.

I'll never be a lap dog, licking dirty feet,
A sleek dog, a meek dog, cringing for my meat.
Not for me the fireside, the well-filled plate,
But shut door, and sharp stone and cuff and kick, and hate.

Not for me the other dogs, running by my side,
Some have run a short while, but none of them would bide.
O mine is still the lone trail, the hard trail the best,
Wide wind, and wild stars and hunger of the quest!

Irene McLeod *Lone Dog*

Bonne année
Globe
Paris
LA TUNISIE
a une importance
stratégique
exceptionnelle
Le contre-torpilleur
gouvernemental
«José-Luis-Diez»
a tenté cette nuit
de forcer le blocus
de la flotte
nationaliste espagnole
Le 4 janvier.
Un procès
monstre
va s'ouvrir
à Berlin

WAGG THE DOG

He is only a small yellow dog and distinctly
a parvenu, so to speak. He never would take a prize
in a dog-show by any chance, because he lacks the two
principal requisites: ancestry and style. He has none of
that high-bred ugliness which is the distinguishing mark
of aristocracy. Still less has he the beauty
of form and face which wins the judges' hearts.
He is nobody in particular, and he doesn't care,
a characteristic, by the way, among men as well as dogs,
which often leads to a philosophical content.

Celie Gaines *Wagg's Protégé*

Be careful that mutt doesn't get into a race with a caterpillar some day and die of heart collapse.

Unknown

I like a bit of a mongrel myself, whether it's a man or a dog: they're the best for everyday.

George Bernard Shaw

ONLY A CUR

And yet within that form uncouth, ungainly,
Are things not always linked to human dust—
Virtues that oft in man we look for vainly—
Courage, affection, faithfulness to trust.

Thomas Dunn *The Selected Poems*

THE BEST MUTT IN NEW YORK

"This leaves," said the judge, "only one dog that we have not considered and found lacking in some detail necessary to the perfect mutt."

Beat-It had just discovered a superb nest of fleas on his shin bone and was scratching them with gusto, so he could not bother to pay attention to what those two-legged ones were saying.

"Will you read out the description of this dog?" said the Chairman of the Judges to the clerk who was busy consulting the entry card.

"Sorry, sir," said the clerk, "it isn't exactly clear, but as far as I can make it out, it is 'Beat-It, entered by John the Junkman, care of Tante Mathilde's Cider Stube, Eleventh avenue near Forty-fourth street.'"

"Honorable Mr. Junkman, ladies and gentlemen," said the judge, lifting a fine silver dog collar and an envelope in his hand, "I have the honor to announce that Beat-It, well-beloved pet of Mr. Junkman, has won first prize as the Best Mutt in New York.

"The points on which this dog is adjudged the winner are the following:

"First—the dog is so dirty that we can't imagine what color he is underneath, and he smells so bad that all of his companions instinctively shun him. This odor is nothing that can be differentiated or accurately described, combining, as it does, garbage cans, street refuse, tar, rubber, dog, and other components that we cannot recognize.

"Second—this dog has the greatest number of fleas of all the dogs present. He has paid no attention to anyone or anything, and devoted his whole time and energy this evening to the removal and consumption of his tormentors.

"Third—the dog has absolutely no identifiable features. His ears do not match and neither of them looks like the ear of any known breed of dog. The same holds true of his tail, his legs, his body, his posture, and the shape of his head. The only thing we are sure of (if we are not mistaken) is that he is a dog. He is dirty. He has fleas. He resembles no known kind of dog. He has bad manners. Therefore, Mr. Junkman, ladies and gentlemen, I take great pleasure in awarding the silver dog-collar and the prize of one hundred dollars to Beat-It, the Best Mutt in New York."

Zhenya and Jan Gay *The Mutt Book*

A REMARKABLE DOG

I well remember a large dog, something of the mastiff kind, and perhaps a mixed breed of the bull-dog. I was one day standing in the street of a large town in the north of England, conversing with a friend, when this animal came up to us, and remained looking up in my face with a most prying and sagacious look. "What," said I, to my friend, "does that dog want? He evidently wants something." "Give him a halfpenny," said he, "and you will see." I gave him the money, and he immediately took it up and marched to a baker's shop close at hand, where he laid it out for a cake.

Ingram Cobbin *Memoirs of My Dog*

THE VAGABONDS

We are two travellers, Roger and I.
Roger's my dog.—Come here, you scamp!
Jump for the gentlemen,—mind your eye!
Over the table,—look out for the lamp!
The rogue is growing a little old;
Five years we've tramped through wind and weather,
And slept out-doors when nights were cold,
And ate and drank—and starved—together.

John Townsend Trowbridge *The Vagabonds*

THE DOG AND THE WOLF

A gaunt Wolf was almost dead with hunger when he happened to meet a House-dog who was passing by.
"Ah, Cousin," said the Dog.
"I knew how it would be; your irregular life will soon be the ruin of you. Why do you not work steadily as I do, and get your food regularly given to you?"
"I would have no objection," said the Wolf, "if I could only get a place."
"I will easily arrange that for you," said the Dog; "Come with me to my master and you shall share my work."
So the Wolf and the Dog went towards the town together.

On the way there the Wolf noticed that the hair on a certain part of the Dog's neck was very much worn away, so he asked him how that had come about.
"Oh, it is nothing," said the Dog. "That is only the place where the collar is put on at night to keep me chained up; it chafes a bit, but one soon gets used to it."
"Is that all?" said the Wolf. "Then good-bye to you, Master Dog."
Better starve free than be a fat slave.

Aesop *The Dog and the Wolf*

A YELLOW DOG

I never knew why in the Western States of America a yellow dog should be proverbially considered the acme of canine degradation and incompetency, nor why the possession of one should seriously affect the social standing of its possessor. But the fact being established, I think we accepted it at Rattlers Ridge without question.

Bret Harte *A Yellow Dog*

I am called a dog because I fawn on those who give me anything, I yelp at those who refuse, and I set my teeth in rascals.

Diogenes

The reason a dog has so
many friends is that he wags
his tail instead of his tongue.

Anonymous

THE ADVENTURES OF TOMMY

He ran madly, but in the shifting, changing crowd he lost sight of the man in the grey coat who had looked so familiar. He had also lost Marie, and was in a quarter totally unknown to him. It was beginning to rain, and the daintily bred dog shivered and picked his way carefully. He looked up inquiringly into the faces of the passers-by, but they took no notice. Someone picked up a stray stone and threw it with sure aim. Tommy was not used to dodging stones, and it hit its mark; he was not a coward, so he did not cry, but with a little whine ran on, limping slightly. The stone had

hurt, but the dull, uncomprehending sense of desolation which crept into the heart of the little animal who, in his short life, had learnt to regard mankind with blind trust and love, hurt far more.

A little farther on a man seized him and roughly dragged off the silver collar, and glanced at it keenly. "Silver, I'll warrant," he said, "and no address, 'Tommy'"—but the dog, rendered cautious, ran on. That night Tommy slept under the arch of a bridge with a dirty tramp, who gave him nevertheless his first kind word and a share of his scanty supper. But they had to part all too soon next day, and without any breakfast either.

Already Tommy had learnt to shrink from notice and to dodge stones and kicks and horses' feet. As he crept along by the side of the street, sniffing vainly at the muddy gutters for that belated breakfast, a policeman caught hold of him; the touch, though rough, was not unkind, and Tommy stood still. "Here's nobody's dog." The man said. "I must take you with me." And to the police station Tommy went. It was a cold, bare room and a scanty meal, but the dog was thankful for the shelter, and slept that day and night out in utter weariness.

Kathleen Blaxter Fuller *The Adventures of Tommy*

ROVER

One pleasant October evening, Arthur Hamilton was at play in front of the small, brown cottage in which he lived. He and his brother James, were having a great frolic with a large spotted dog, who was performing a great variety of antics, such as only well-educated dogs understand. But Rover had been carefully initiated into the mysteries of making a bow while standing on his hind legs, tossing pieces of bread off his nose, putting up his fore-paws with a most imploring look, and piteous whine, which the boys called "begging for money," and when a chip had been given him, he uttered a most energetic bow-wow-wow, which they regarded as equivalent to "thank you, sir," and walked off.

Anonymous *Arthur Hamilton and his Dog*

LOST DOGS

Why is it that my heart is so touched whenever I meet a dog lost in our noisy streets? Why do I feel such anguished pity when I see one of these creatures coming and going, sniffing everyone, frightened, despairing of even finding its master?

Émile Zola

ROUGHING IT

He is always poor, out of luck and friendless. The meanest creatures despise him, and even the fleas would desert him for a velocipede. He is so spiritless and cowardly that even while his exposed teeth are pretending a threat, the rest of his face is apologizing for it. And he is so homely!—so scrawny, and ribby, and coarse-haired, and pitiful.

Mark Twain *Roughing It*

OLD DOGS

Old dogs, like old shoes, are comfortable. They might be a bit out of shape and a little worn around the edges, but they fit well.

Bonnie Willcox

The truth I do not stretch or shove
When I state the dog is full of love.
I've also proved, by actual test,
A wet dog is the lovingest.

Ogden Nash

SKIP

About two in the morning we both heard a sharp bark downstairs and knew it was Skip, anxious to be let in. So down I went and opened the portico, and Skip simply scuttled in and up to Archie's room, where Archie waked up enough to receive literally with open arms and then went to sleep cuddled up to him.

Theodore Roosevelt

TYKE, THE LITTLE MUTT

"I don't think there is any use in trying at that big house on the hill," said the crow.

"Why not?" asked the little dog. "You say they have lots of dogs, so why wouldn't they like to have me, too?"

"Because," said the crow, "all those dogs are fancy dogs; they are hunting dogs and shepherd dogs and show dogs, and from what I see of you I don't think you are any special kind of dog at all."

"I don't know whether I am or not," said the little dog. "I have never had anyone to tell me what kind of dog I am. For all I know, I might be a hunting dog or I might be a terrier or I might be a very special kind of breed."

"Not likely," said the crow. "I think you are just a little mutt, and you will have to make the best of it."

Dorothy K. L'Hommedieu *Tyke, the Little Mutt*

SHARIK

The street lamps were alight all along Prechistenka Street. His flank hurt unbearably, but for the moment Sharik forgot about it, absorbed by a single thought: how to avoid losing sight of this miraculous fur-coated vision in the hurly-burly of the storm and how to show him his love and devotion. Seven times along the whole length of Prechistenka Street as far as the cross-roads at Obukhov Street he showed it. At Myortvy Street he kissed his boot, he cleared the way by barking at a lady and frightened her into falling flat on the pavement, and twice he gave a howl to make sure the gentleman still felt sorry for him.

A filthy, thieving stray torn cat slunk out from behind a drainpipe and despite the snowstorm, sniffed the Cracower. Sharik went blind with rage at the thought that this rich eccentric who picked up injured dogs in doorways might take pity on this robber and make him share the sausage. So he bared his teeth so fiercely that the cat, with a hiss like a leaky hosepipe, shinned back up the drainpipe right to the second floor. Grrrr! Woof! Gone! We can't go handing out Moscow State groceries to all the strays loafing about Prechistenka Street.

Mikhail Bulgakov *Heart of a Dog*

THE MONGREL OF SOMERSTOWN

There are a great many dogs in shy neighbourhoods, who keep boys. I have my eye on a mongrel in Somerstown who keeps three boys. He feigns that he can bring down sparrows, and unburrow rats (he can do neither), and he takes the boys out on sporting pretences into all sorts of suburban fields. He has likewise made them believe that he possesses some mysterious knowledge of the art of fishing, and they consider themselves incompletely equipped for the Hampstead ponds, with a pickle-jar and wide-mouthed bottle, unless he is with them and barking tremendously.

Charles Dickens *The Uncommercial Traveller*

BONES

If Bones generally exhibited no preference for any particular individual in camp, he always made an exception in favor of drunkards. Even an ordinary roistering bacchanalian party brought him out from under a tree or a shed in the keenest satisfaction. He would accompany them through the long straggling street of the settlement, barking his delight at every step or misstep of the revelers, and exhibiting none of that mistrust of eye which marked his attendance upon the sane and the respectable. He accepted even their uncouth play without a snarl or a yelp, hypocritically pretending even to like it; and I conscientiously believe would have allowed a tin can to be attached to his tail if the hand that tied it on were only unsteady, and the voice that bade him "lie still" were husky with liquor. He would "see" the party cheerfully into a saloon, wait outside the door—his tongue fairly lolling from his mouth in enjoyment—until they reappeared, permit them even to tumble over him with pleasure, and then gambol away before them, heedless of awkwardly projected stones and epithets. He would afterward accompany them separately home, or lie with them at crossroads until they were assisted to their cabins. Then he would trot rakishly to his own haunt by the saloon stove, with the slightly conscious air of having been a bad dog, yet of having had a good time.

Bret Harte *A Yellow Dog*

CRAB THE DOG

"O, 'tis a foul thing when a cur cannot keep himself in all companies! I would have, as one should say, one that takes upon him to be a dog indeed, to be, as it were, a dog at all things. If I had not had more wit than he, to take a fault upon me that he did, I think verily he had been hanged for't; … Nay, I'll be sworn, I have sat in the stocks for puddings he hath stolen, otherwise he had been executed; I have stood on the pillory for geese he hath killed, otherwise he had suffered for't. Thou thinkest not of this now."

William Shakespeare *Two Gentlemen of Verona*

PETE

"as for his pretensions to being a thoroughbred
i take no stock in them
i asked a flea of his about it
recently and the flea said
i doubt peters claim to aristocracy
very much he does not look like
an aristocrat to me

and more than that he does not taste like one
i have bit some pretty swell dogs
in my time and i ought to know
if pete is an aristocrat
then i am a bengal tiger
but in hard times like these
a flea has got to put up with
any kind of dog he can get hold of"

Don Marquis *A Radical Flea*

Launce: "Marry, sir, I carried Mistress Silvia the dog you bade me."

Proteus: "And what says she to my little jewel?"

Launce: "Marry, she says, your dog was a cur, and tells you, currish thanks is good enough for such a present."

William Shakespeare *Two Gentlemen of Verona*

FOUR FEET

I have done mostly what most men do,
And pushed it out of my mind;
But I can't forget, if I wanted to,
Four-Feet trotting behind.

Day after day, the whole day through—
Wherever my road inclined—
Four-Feet said, "I'm coming with you!"
And trotted along behind.

Now I must go by some other round,
Which I shall never find—
Somewhere that does not carry the sound
Of Four-Feet trotting behind.

Rudyard Kipling *Four Feet*

THE STORY OF A MONGREL

What a cold, dreary, November day!

But that was only in the better parts. How did the great London underworld fare in such weather? Let us see. Up yonder alley off the big street the wind sweeps up the dirty cobbles, the old draughty houses creak and groan as if each rattle would be their last. A poor, wretched child is huddled up against a wall, while a little further down the narrow street a little dog is seeking the shelter of a doorstep. What a day!

As evening approached, the wind, rain and misery increased. Even the miserable child had at last returned to his home and the dog was left alone on the doorstep. He was a mongrel, is a mongrel, and ever will be a mongrel, though at least a mongrel of character.

Moyra Charlton *Patch: the Story of a Mongrel*

MONTMORENCY'S MISSION

Montmorency's ambition in life, is to get in the way and be sworn at. If he can squirm in anywhere where he particularly is not wanted, and be a perfect nuisance, and make people mad, and have things thrown at his head, then he feels his day has not been wasted.

Jerome K. Jerome *Three Men in a Boat*

PICTURE CREDITS

TEXT CREDITS

INDEX OF AUTHORS

Published by MQ Publications Limited

12 The Ivories
6–8 Northampton Street
London, N1 2HY
Tel: +44 (0)20 7359 2244
Fax: +44 (0)20 7359 1616
E-mail: mail@mqpublications.com

North American Office
49 West 24th Street
New York, NY 10010
E-mail: information@mqpublicationsus.com

Web site: www.mqpublications.com

ISBN: 1-84601-103-5
978-1-84601-103-0

1 3 5 7 9 0 8 6 4 2

Every effort has been made to contact current copyright holders. Any omission is
unintentional and the publishers would be pleased to hear from any copyright holders
not acknowledged.

Printed in China